ghosts

Ghosts

Siobhan Harvey

OTAGO UNIVERSITY PRESS
Te Whare Tā o Te Wānanga o Ōtākou

*This book is dedicated to the memory of
Sister Pauline (1922–2019) &
Peter (1950–2019)*

Published by Otago University Press
Te Whare Tā o Te Wānanga o Ōtākou
533 Castle Street
Dunedin, New Zealand
university.press@otago.ac.nz
www.otago.ac.nz/press

First published 2021
Copyright © Siobhan Harvey
The moral rights of the author have been asserted.

ISBN 978-1-98-859298-5

Published with the assistance of Creative New Zealand

ARTS COUNCIL OF NEW ZEALAND *TOI AOTEAROA*

Editor: Emma Neale
Cover photograph: 'The Ghost at Braemar Hotel, Auckland' by Liz March, © Siobhan
Harvey 2020

Printed in China through Asia Pacific Offset

MIX
Paper from
responsible sources
FSC® C136333

Contents

Prologue

Night, a Place of Regeneration

Deep with all it buries, the night begins
the story again: the one about our evolution;
the one we're forced to repeat ... Reborn,
the moon sings of the earth, as the soul
sings of the body. Ripples across the skin
of darkness, owl, bittern and black cormorant
offer refrain. Here is music gentle as a breeze:
trees tremble; clouds keep time. The tide turns
in the estuary. A boat rocks a luckless fisherman
to forty winks, his line in need of miracle. A shiver
of sharks nurse their pups, while in the shallows
eels and sea slaters stir. Soul haunting its space,
a writer watches the night
                                        unfold. As if on paper
invisible to the eye, an elegy writes its sorrow
into the shadows. Freed from its foundations,
a house rises like a ghost. Those asleep wake to
outcry ... *Community not opportunity!*, *Give us back*
our homes! ... sirens and teargas, upset vehicles ablaze.
Candles, a vigil; activists are pallbearers as – abracadabra! –
levitation engineered, the house floats into slumbering
sky. Here is evidence of why loss is an inevitable
part of the story: the one about our evolution;
the one we're forced to repeat ... Displaced by
evictions, silhouettes of stealth, families leave
keys under doormats, teapots cooling and beds
unmade, lug belongings
                                        elsewhere. New houses –
million-dollar prices, panoramic views – idle for
owners, life-stories nearly complete. Almost forgotten
in the drama are those who fought distant wars, settled
here after D-day to build something new. Unnoticed
sentinels, they are the departed who endure, spirit-
activists who stand their ground. In harmony,
the last hour of night passes

                                    as the day begins
the story again, light with all it reveals. Reborn,
the sun sings of the earth, as the heart
sings of the body. Ripples across the skin
of daybreak, kingfisher, heron and spoonbill
offer refrain. Here is music calm as a cat's-paw:
clouds tremble; trees keep time. The tide turns
in the estuary. A boat rocks a luckless fisherman
to forty winks, his line in need of miracle. A fever
of stingrays feed in the creek, while in the shallows
crabs and sea worms stir. Soul haunting its space,
a writer watches the day
                              break. As if an echo
silent to the ear, they retreat to the sanctuary of
their imagination. The one about our evolution;
the one we're forced to repeat: here is the story
they create and rewrite
                              into poems such as this.

All the Buildings that Never Were

*The more enlightened our houses are, the more
their walls ooze ghosts.*

ITALO CALVINO

Ghosts

All the buildings that never were.
All the novels unwritten. All the dead

bodies of portraits never realised. The soul-
mates never kissed. Like smoke, this loss –

an invocation of *what if, what if* – lingers
in the air as our ghosts seep into the walls

where they live. Sometimes fleeting glimpses
snatched at midnight when we're sleepless, they

haunt dark corridors where photographs hang;
or rooms where, old wallpaper, they decorate

the heart of the home. But mostly, they are lost
to us, like old lovers who promised passion and eternity

rings which never materialised. Or they are friends
never communicated with, never forgiven. Still our ghosts

exist for what is and what remains, their disembodied
faces watching over us from pictures of prize-giving,

childhoods gone and funerals as we drift through
our thin lives, as if they're illusory, as if they're real.

The Home is Made of Many Souls

It rises and retreats
It fills and clears
It's water
It's a canoe, a clipper, a 737
It's a migrant
It's all travellers
who have taken refuge here
It's a spacesuit,
the body turned alien and alone
It's a gathering
of astronomical bodies
It's the twilight,
early morning and midday
It's the dawn chorus
It's twig, reed and feather
It's the whole placed
carefully in the shade.

Haunted House

At night, the home turns to dark matter:
constellations spin at dusty windows; stray
cats prowl a lightless street; veiled vehicles

steal by. Belonging here is seized
from TV flickers, the home electric with
transmitted crisis, the world-views of

politicians, people-traffickers, wall-builders,
warmongers and fake-news profiteers, ghosts
in the haunted house of the news.

The swell high in the estuary close by,
the home imagines itself, like the migrant,
rowing in ocean air beneath moonlight.

There is upset. There is unsettlement.
Freighted with loss, a sleepwalker disturbs
corridors; their breath troubles empty rooms.

The home soothes this free spirit with warm tea,
guides it back to bed, then sings it to sleep.

Soon thoughts become dead bodies
washed up on starless shores, craft capsized
in deep waters, babies born to detention centres.

The home peels away the roof of this
strange reality, as if it's a scar, as if it bleeds.

At the heart of the matter is such music
as beats in the body unseen, and here the home

calls out sanctuary to all who are displaced, all ghosts
turned away, in dark matter, from entry elsewhere.

Come to me, it cries.
Come be bodies safe as homes

no politician, people-trafficker, wall-builder,
warmonger or fake-news profiteer can haunt.

The Empty House Considered as a Ghost

Rooms robbed of electricity are a body
emptied of power, an apparition.

It has been this way for months, stagnation
unseen by neighbours even as lightning broke

fierce summer afternoons, and stars forked
cool, cloudless nights. See how the bleak sky

tonight trembles with anticipation like a line
dropped into deep water by a luckless fisherman.

See how the empty house creaks upon its joints.
Hear it set free a suffocated cry. The house is

a writer awaiting inspiration for a last word,
the elegy conceived long ago. The house is

a stage abandoned by cast and audience,
direction absent, the curtain about to fall.

Look inside at the shadows, the puppetry
composing an ensemble of distortions: silhouettes

of those who passed their time here once.
The teenager doing the Twist in her bedroom

to a dead radio. The mother weeping close
to the threshold for four sons taken by war. Such spirit

as is still present, but simply overlooked
like a gravestone. The course of the future is set:

a cortège of protestors demanding the house remains;
a procession of police officers, a bulwark; the strain

of an articulated lorry bearing the building elsewhere.
But for now, the eyes – windows – are vacant

in neighbours' faces, as if the house is no longer
part of them, a figure shrouded on a bed of land.

Land

A child dances alone
in the street. A rainbow
arcs the sky. A hawk
circles, descends. A helicopter
appears. Dark-suited, new ghosts
of developers materialise from
the clouds. Here visions –
wild places to shelter –
are set upon empty land
by the writer's eye.

Once the all-seeing water carried
dreams to this safe shore: liquid
stars to navigate the ancients;
shallows to nurse great whites;
coastline to settle waders' Arctic flight;
sea views for soldiers arriving home.

Now this land is gifted to the gods
of helicopters, SUVs, M6s, shark-nosed
disruptors who conjure the mantra of
mixed model, urban renewal, WOW factor,
solar gain, waterfront living. There's money
to summon – ta-da! – from soil. Everything
seen or imagined belongs to them. The past –
its evicted, protestors and peacemakers –
is a trick, an adjunct made to disappear.

As if it's the scattering of birds
into late morning, the shriek of
banshees escapes; the helicopter too.

The displaced need this land to live.
They want their future to grow here,
like trees. They want their children

to dance upon it alone, to feel sap
pulse through the branch; rainbow

and hawk to rise from it. This close
to regeneration, the evicted lament
that which they cannot settle,
cannot own. Their wailing is –
the rustle of money, whisperings
of the past – almost quelled;
almost, but not quite.

Rise Up

Like the candlelight of protestors, the fires
cast from old homes upon the inlet's dark water
are extinguished by eviction. Darkness
may consume them, they who are ghosts,
who are displaced from their homes, power
cut, emptied of belongings perhaps, but
these protestors are alight with oxygen
enough to flame protest, *Rise Up! Rise Up!*

Like a symphony on the theme of loss,
their voice carries across the land.
It is owl cry. It is moonlight. By night,
it is breath disturbing those who sleep.
Rise Up! Rise Up! Their chant swells again
with the tide. As homes are taken to resting
elsewhere, these protestors are left to watch
from windows dead without their fire.

Like electricity, the pulse of rejection burns
long in them. It is a fierce sun. It is the last song
of a dying bird. And they who are incandescent
with injustice, continue their cry. *Rise Up! Rise Up!*
For these protestors have nothing but embers,
yet they fight on with a burning need for home,
family and faith, if only to retain their voice.
Which is the most powerful thing of all.

New Developments

Let others live in the past.
For the developers, it is settled,
made extinct; except in the mind

of the trapped where life lingers
in the shadows of what might be.
The developers are inspired by

the flux found in the world, natural
in its upheaval. Shift of the sun, east
to west, across the ether. The airy wax

and wane of the moon. Gentle whirl
of constellation in the night sky. Ebb
and flow of the tide. Changes

in the weather, instant as lightning.
They measure progress in movement,
displacement and regeneration.

In steel roofs and windows, new
walls and doors, developers magic
concrete miracles from empty space,

capital gain from asset loss.
It's a matter of belief. The future
as new developments, new disruptors;

no dereliction or abandonment.
They spin everything else,
like homelessness and loss,

into a feel-good story, as if
those who built community
can be written out of it, cast off
as antediluvian, as a failure to adapt.

Requiem for a War, with Refrain

(a duet for developer and protestor)

Not past but present
Not present but protest
Not protest but asset
Not asset but upset
Not upset but redevelopment
Not redevelopment but real developments
Not real developments but housing shortage
Not housing shortage but sanctuary
Not sanctuary but opportunity
Not opportunity but community

Not community but tax credit
Not tax credit but security
Not security but eviction
Not eviction but action
Not action but auction
Not auction but exploitation
Not exploitation but economics
Not economics but envy
Not envy but opportunity
Not opportunity but community

Not community but gravy train
Not gravy train but tīpuna
Not tīpuna but trickle down
Not trickle down but safety net
Not safety net but progress
Not progress but political redress
Not political redress but freewill and freehold
Not freewill or freehold but family
Not family but opportunity
Not opportunity but community

The Poem of the Short Film of the Story of the House

1937: Prime Minister Savage opens the first state house

'Action!' the director says
and, a door open to a new day,
the first seconds of film alight
upon the lead. Stout, modest:
the state house is, like its auteur,
a character actor thrust – champion
of the common man – into the spotlight.

Think Wallace Beery.
Think Marie Dressler.
Think Charles Laughton.

As if from a paper-thin stage,
it delivers simple lines, offers
itself with little adornment.
These speak of a backstory:
war; recession; poverty;
the need to look within
for solutions, to make –
as if a new building –
the future a better place.

For a moment, imagine it
as no movie, as empty
space, derelict land,
the story of the house
dismantled, unrealised.

With a ghostly chill,
the director orders, 'Cut!'
And his housing programme ends.

Where would the audience be?

Where they are now perhaps,
with the film no longer playing,
no new scenes appearing
to show homeless families
sleeping in cars, mass evictions.

Let this not be
forgotten: the house
is a star of mass productions.
Let the audience return to it.
Let the fourth wall break,
the director take centre-stage.
Let all raise the spectre of
the community besieged
as the story of the house,
slight legacy, quickly fades.

Erasure

January 2015: Prime Minister Key announces 8000 state homes to be sold off by 2017

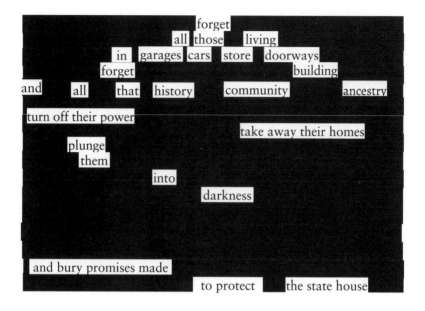

forget
all those living
in garages cars store doorways
forget building
and all that history community ancestry

turn off their power

take away their homes

plunge
them

into

darkness

and bury promises made

to protect the state house

Spell Spoken upon the Destruction of a Home

Let the young stray wild as ghosts

Let the parents live, like echoes, in the space between breaths

Let the ancestors exist, like vacant land, in the gulf between worlds

Let their voices shatter like those broken in protest

Let their bodies desiccate like dust, like earth

Let their rooms, ripe with memories, burst open like bad fruit

Let their windows bleed and scar, like wounds

Let their roofs be recycled into new cars, new property

Let one of them forget their origins

Let one of them be educated at Harvard

Let one of them be reinvented as merchant banker or politician

Let one of them harden their heart against those who gave shelter, sanctuary and love

Serving Notice upon the Prime Minister

An amendment to 1986 Residential Tenancies Act

Relating to a state house (definition: *a house owned by the State*) located at 260 Tinakori Road, Wellington

Section 51   Termination by notice

(1)   Subject to **Sections 52, 53, 53A, 59** and **59A,** the minimum period of notice required to be given by we, the evicted, to terminate the tenancy of 260 Tinakori Road, Wellington, shall be as follows:

> (a) where we, the evicted, owners of all state houses require all state houses as the principal place of residence for we, the evicted or any members of our whānau, 42 days:
> (b) where we, the evicted, use state houses, or have acquired state houses, for occupation by our neighbours, that fact being clearly stated in the tenancy agreement of 260 Tinakori Road, Wellington, 42 days:
> (c) where we, the evicted, give vacant possession of 260 Tinakori Road, Wellington, to a new tenant, 42 days.

(2)   Subject to **Sections 52, 53, 53A, 59** and **59A,** where we, the evicted, have given an effective notice to terminate the tenancy of 260 Tinakori Road, Wellington, we, the evicted, may at any time before the expiry of the notice enforce immediate termination of that tenancy where actions undertaken by the Prime Minister, or that party's agents are shown to have misled or affected unjustly the interests of we, the evicted.

(3)   Subject to **Sections 52, 53, 53A, 59** and **59A,** where we, the evicted, have given an effective notice to terminate the tenancy of 260 Tinakori Road, Wellington, the Prime Minister or that party's agents are obliged to notice that they are on notice.

(4)   Subject to **Sections** 52, 53, 53A, 59 and 59A, every notice to terminate the tenancy of 260 Tinakori Road, Wellington, shall:

(a) be in writing, in voice, in debate, in marching, in banner waving, in hīkoi, in referendum, in voting and/or in blood; and

(b) identify the Prime Minister and that party's agents to which it relates; and

(c) specify the date by which the Prime Minister and that party's agents are to vacate 260 Tinakori Road, Wellington; and

(d) be signed in writing, in voice, in debate, in marching, in banner waving, in hīkoi, in referendum, in voting and/or in blood by we, the evicted.

Ghost Stories

We need ghost stories because we, in fact, are the ghosts.

STEPHEN KING

The Evicted

Erase our sky. Expose us
to different weather, the topographies of
clouds, stars, storms and eclipses seen
from the perspective of the unfamiliar
suburbs built for us by eviction, in spite
of our joy at the rain, twilight, thunder
and blood moons of where we were.

Move us miles by all means. Take away
our tongues, our waiata, our pūrākau,
our tala, our hiva kakala. Let them carry
their music into others' settled lives.

A pittance for our homes. May they become
new blankets for babies, books for students, dreams
for young lovers and worn out armchairs for the elderly,
even as our gardens are trampled, and our community
is hocked off to highest bidder: *going … going … gone!*

Like stock, trade us down
to glass-coffined lobbies, to flights
of Lego stairs, to empty flats. Let us live
on top of our neighbours. Let us live
out our days staring at the flowers
on walls you've gifted us. The air
conditioner and security alarm are tricks,
like water gushing from silver taps
into stainless sinks, like gold dust falling
from 'cool white' eco bulbs in every room.

Our feet are cold on the tiled floors laid out for us
like welcoming mats, when all we ever wanted was
matai, kauri and tawa to grow strong beside us,
their canopies enough to picnic beneath.

Remember wherever you leave us,
our tables will overflow with fish and bread
enough to feed all our gatherings.

Remember our children grow
like sunflowers. Like solar panels,
they soak up the warmth
our love gives them, for tomorrow
they *will* take back our sky.

Ghost Stories

We are raised by the air
from empty neighbourhood,

overcrowded inner-city,
open space, ocean,

new land and old
story; everywhere.

The blue of us
isn't sadness, but strength

of atmosphere.
The white of us

isn't scared, but softness
of snow. The black of us

isn't our downfall,
but the power of matter

forever present,
yet as unseen

as the seismic,
sonic and soul.

We commune whenever
there's breath and belief.

We trace wherever
pen touches paper:

spirited sheet,
parchment thin and inky eyed;

ill character,
bleakly written and bad blood;

haunting
and spellbound.

Always we enchant
life with our life,

keen in our craving
to make everyone like us.

The Ghosts of East Berlin

After their sudden closure at midnight on 13 August 1962,
stations on the East Berlin transport system became known as
ghosts.

We are memories no one can erase.
Like the contours of a map, we
trace an unreal landscape. Still life
haunts us, as if double agent
or bad luck. Now we've cracked,
secrets spilled like so much hidden
meaning – network of informants; arbitrary
detention; forced disappearance; death.

The moon high, derelict at midnight,
we are witnessed again as if an emptiness
of embassies, a concentration of gulags
or a desertion of outposts. A second
for us to emanate the rattle of old chains,
their chime and clinker, our missing links.
Then the light fades and, Babushka,
the eye swallows us again.

The Ghosts of Wall Unbuilt

Spook not yet realised,
earth alive with the slight
of this existence, ghosts already
trespass the land and indefensible sky.

We hang in the heavens,
a kaleidoscope of monarchs, orange
as late autumn leaves, amber
lights or sparks. Stirred by electricity
unplugged, ours is a 3000-mile flight,
not of the illegal, but of those free
as the wind. Here we settle
to citrus blossom and red soil,
a peaceful resistance against
Green Cards, phantom jobs
in Walmart and cheap cars.

Bodies shimmering like stars,
we are keen to consume
different dreams, cusp-laden
as chrysalids: new ghosts
to trace their parents' lives
backwards, like being reborn.

This is our language of escape,
universal as instinct or need,
a million wings conversant in
how to belong everywhere
and nowhere like the word
'migrant' and the word 'wall'.

Let us remain in place of a broken promise.
Let our promise remain in this unbroken place,

erasing segregation and shame as an ecosystem
of survival, healing, tolerance and hope.

The Ghosts of Singapore

2001–2006, Bidadari Cemetery, Singapore: 126,000 graves dug up to free land for new roads, houses, malls and an underground.

Now it's the time for the living
to excavate the dead. Those who dwell in
our memories. Those who we worship
are reborn. The wise who transcend
silence with their undying love.

For we are the compelled, interred
and unearthed. Tight as boxes,
our homes convey us until last
breath, a pocket of air resting
upon another, another … all
raised high into the sky as if
there is shelter. We need
new land to grow, fresh
as a forest, for our offspring
must know lives beyond ours,
so they can raise newborns.

Each plot opens up to us,
the bystanders, as if the solemn
voice of the soil is freed from
an earthly mouth, a grave scar.

And the sky turns to crimson
sunbirds, flocks of the disturbed
singing an elegy to the outcast,
while we are moved by the discovery
of a stray bone or tooth, when all else is
dust, is – a miracle – housed by the air.

Soon we'll treasure caskets
of small remains. We'll rest
them in new homes. The future

and the past reconciled in them,
they will watch over us
whenever we fall asleep.

The Ghosts of Manus Regional Processing Centre

What if we are castaway
from our origins, so floated
to a fear of outsiders, we forget
the exiles who created us?

What if we are imprisoned
by an idea, made soulless
in its isolating effect, and how –
as if magic – it displaces the alien?

What if we are invisible
to their compassion, ghosts
of their ghosts, and home
is a place which no longer exists?

Would we look inwards, like the broken
detained in the house of the absent heart?

Would we gaze outwards, like the dreamer
held on an island of endless ocean?

Would our arms stretch across the deep?
Would our courage break down that wall,
embrace the other life we find there?

Would this humanity set us free?
Would this humanity return our souls?

The Ghosts of Aranui

for Mr D

The evicted; the exiled; the gone:
the land remains alive with them,
like shadows, shudders or warmth
of the sun. When light bulbs flicker.
When ornaments dance and TVs whirr.
When actors, captive to drama, disappear.
So, an invisible engine, another tremor
rolls through our homes. And we,
the enduring, stand in doorways searching
for signs of the departed and lost
in broken earth and sky faint with starlight.

Everywhere we see the realisation of time
hauling itself back in: daylight retreating
to darkness; abandoned sections recomposing
the rubble of weatherboard and glass, broken
blankets, into safe places to live; the façades
of the collapsed peering at us like strangers
with paralysis. Here our minds are returned

to kids playing in the street, birdsong
and lawns being mowed. The devastation
of sinkage, Portaloo and liquefaction is
invisible in the memory of hard work,
benefits, hand-me-downs and gangs,
where the edges of our overlooked lives
once gathered, as families, in state homes.

Now we're left alone with our reflections,
we shiver like aftershocks, like those awake
to forgotten memories, as we imagine
we might be as we once were.

Orphan Gifts

We always return to our ancestors.
See our grandmother's veins rise
on the back of our hand. See
our mother's face in every mirror,

every reflection of the dead. But
it's the mystery ones, absent
and unloved ones erased
from birth certificates – fathers,

grandfathers – whose lives, shadow
worlds, we inhabit. Their names are
Unknown. They christen space obscure
as fog. They saturate us with words silenced

by our questions, so we remain unanswered
by the tongues they gave us. Starched bodies
imprisoned in photographs they might be,
but we'll never see them, never touch their past

selves slight as a fingertip's caress. Exposure
to dementia, arthritis and heart failure:
these are the ill-written bequests
doctors will announce on their behalf.

So we turn to our orphan gifts:
our soul-nourishing need to write
about the secret lives of characters;
the vessels we, born landlocked, helm

with an ease worthy of ancient discoverers;
the way we venture wildly upon horses,
as if somewhere within we learned to ride.
Here are such confessions as go unheard

by us. Here, as if exorcising demons,
pests in the home, or old companions
we are now stranger to, our ancestors
rest easy in our hidden embrace.

Caesura

Upon the death of wasps

We watch at windows we cannot open,
seal the doors with wax, we think,

and revel in the wonder of these imperfect speakers,
as tooth of wolf and tongue of dog, witch's maw

and adder's fork, owlet's wing and lizard's leg,
resmethrin, eye of newt and tetrachloroethylene

bubble in our cauldron close by. We stir
with wickedness, not wanting this swarm

to drive us from our home. Our cure creeps
everywhere, slick as burnt sugar, blocks noses

as if nests, turns hands to pumping. Again
and again. As though bailing out a sinking ship,

not scuttling one. As though raising water
to end a fire, not lighting the flames.

And while a city burns, cinders falling
all jade and topaz, we play a violin

concerto, as if from a villa in Antium.
Our tune turns their home, all spit and polish,

rancid with decay. Seeing the victims swaddled
in mortuary bands, we ask if we can excuse our actions

by claiming greater intelligence or more right to life?
No. Our happiness springs from open windows

and knowing that whispers of the unwelcome
have been brought to an end. Now

it's too late to experiment with the truth.
A day of death has passed, and silence –

like dust, scum or the eggs of ants –
clings to our walls, clings to our air.

To the Graves

Come read *I, Claudius*
and *No More Ghosts* as we
who picnic here upon wild fruit
and cold meat are sated by
our memories, and the sun –
blind to the night that comes
to all – bears down with
an intensity we no longer
feel; a bough yielding
to its fate, blossoms
long fallen, crop hung
and blackened like bats, we
keep company with the tomb-
stones of others, our family
and those who slump frail
flowers before us, unearthed
from overgrown plots, extract
secrets kept from priests, confess
lives they think we've missed –
the birth of a child; a good omen
in the tea leaves; a shock diagnosis –
or recite a familiar passage then
make for home emptied of
their burdens as the light
fails and dusk comes quick
as a stroke, an odd sensation,
fingertip faint, of someone
shadowing, a blight of
pain buried deep,
or a last breath.

Ghost Music

after Robert Graves

By breath carried
from the bellows,
as if the lungs
of this organ,
as if the larynx
of this instrument,
there rises
in lead arteries,
the lifeblood of
the composition,
revealing a spirit
note – and more –
that haunts
the air like
a chorus
conducted
in ether,
a séance
of spectres
singing
               out
among the living
who congregate
in communion
with the ghost
who they know
speaks to them
from within,
here is a divine
mystery or other
worldly moment
made manifest
which lifts

        the soul

            somewhere

                else.

My Ghosts Rise Up in Lockdown

In Lockdown, they rise up, free
at last to roam the dim corridors

and empty rooms of home. My mind
is a place as forsaken as the wild

earth, forest, foreshore and ocean
forgotten by those in isolation. Here

my ghosts burst their bubbles, return
to me all I've long sought to misplace:

broken relationships with parents, always
distant, always pained; tortured lovers

who summon the past in fitful bursts,
punches to the gut; the countless dead,

lost ancestors I never got to know. Breath
upon the back of the neck, they are; blood

collecting at open wound. Cut like
time, my restless ghosts move me

to Level 3. Gatherings en masse, they
let their sterile bodies – hollow eyes,

rotten skins, weeping sores – loose
to the light. In this, an epiphany:

the meaningful divide between experience
and memory is loss. Almost, I fix them

with chemicals, but remnants are deadened
to taxidermic display. Realisation doesn't last.

Once more cut like time, my ghosts dislocate me
to Level 2, become animated as silent film stars,

viscera close to the surface, until they float again
across the negative of my mind, the latent rendered

insensitive to further illumination. Now winter
sets them solid, days of doing nothing turn

them harder than the heart, and I become another
kind of ghost, wretch of all I remember, all I forget.

My Invisible Remains

Now I know what a ghost is. Unfinished business, that's what.

SALMAN RUSHDIE

Building Memories

a sequence

i: My First Memory is a Room

It has walls, my memory, dark and determined as
the workings of a watch. Its movement is captured
in light, a broken blind. The locked door is a mouth
from which screams can't escape. The freestanding
fridge, tall as a casket, stares it down. A pale body
confined to the ceiling is a cloud turning
this room, this memory into the sky, and I
hang in the shadows, solid as a ghost, seeing
this memory, this room make sense of what unfolds
and how the floor – antiseptic clean; asymmetrical,
stepping-stone tiles – is a jigsaw ...
                                   piece of
time, swollen as a punch, moves this memory,
this room on. *IhateyouIhateyouIhateyou!* Quickening,
a body – shadow, spirited – looms over me. Still
the cloud, meek girl, circles the ceiling,
and this room, this memory and I turn to
face one another, embrace; we *will* get through this,
we say. Then we are sent flying. Not shapeshifters,
not Alcyone, Leda or Hecate, not even moons, we
spin through space, set to freestanding, and always
I move forwards with this memory, this room.

ii: My Second Memory is a Duplex

Tight and narrow. Thin-
walled. The noise of
neighbours, other memories,
barks in upon this. *Bad dog!*
No escaping the unleashed:
remembrance of being locked into
hunched space, hungry, fierce
heat of high summer, afternoon
light full, the father gone
to nightshift, turning of
his lathe tirelessly through
the coming dark, and the mother
abandoned to squabbling
kids, to exercising the hound,
and her temper. All the energy of
my five-year-old body resists
being still, not even when bolted
door opens on this squat space,
Get to sleep! The dog snarls; the strap
is set free. The memory owned
by this duplex hunts the mother
back to the kitchen, *Bad dog!*
slinks in the corner, rage
of the radio turned high
to hungry wails with news
of the cruel weather, forecasts
for an ongoing depression
and how – a mindset, really,
a confined space – there's more
of everything bad to come.

iii: My Third Memory is a Bungalow

Looking back, this memory is a single storey, the view coffined
from cement blocks, grey sky, low light and I – clothed in
second-hand, diminutive and alone – shrink to the raised
voices at my back, *I can't take this hellhole any more!* as leaves,
dead red, fall from trees, and I become closed, like her suitcase,
into this memory on repeat, this space reduced to a single outlook
as if I'm forever trapped here by her exit, and I'm always to blame,
because she would be complete if I wasn't broken, wasn't the mistake,
unplanned, she has to reject to be herself, entire and alone; and so
I'm left to hear a slammed door echo through my future, as a memory
of the day she abandoned me and, body cowered before a tight pane,
I watched her go, her shadow an ever-diminishing thing.

iv: My Fourth Memory is Semi-Detached

It survives beside the others,
this memory, resident of
the lives I didn't choose:
semi-
        detached,
I'm a stay-at-home
mum married at eighteen
to a man I met at school,
two kids, two Minis, pets;
semi-
        detached,
I'm confined
to two-up, two-down, safety
found in small spaces like
a neighbour's inner-life,
part-time job at Poundland,
boarding-house holiday in Rhyl;
semi-
        detached,
I'm too close
to the cast off, broken
toys, broken bones
which build each day
in my parents' half-house
of kaleidoscope pieces –
bright and dark; not quite,
semi-
        detached,
I'm torn
by these memories,
exile of the in-between:
for which are made thin
as fabric, and which are real
things settled for when
semi-
        detached?

v: My Fifth Memory is Detached

Here we're unhinged.
Not a family unit, this
memory is a place apart.
Room at the top, I
am a closed door,
am a reckoning with
absence, with sound, am screams
below, am the one to blame
when others break windows,
argue, tear, punch, bruise large
as a mother's fist. Hardened
by moonlight, I brood
about the loose
                                    threats
to section me to a madhouse,
mother howling my name
as I lose myself in

> *A Place to Go*
> *A Kind of Loving*
> *Look Back in Anger*

in all the kitchen-sink dramas
of not eating and drugs
and suicide and homelessness
and finding a break in education,
its promise of escape. To separate
ourselves from those who raise us
is a fate no child should face alone.
The memory it constructs severs
the owner from the act as if
they're an abandoned figure
confined to a locked room
in an empty house
detached.

vi: My Last Memory is Home

Forever, as I leave you,
my last memory of home
remains. Like the revenant,
it's built of things already lost:
white sheet out in bad weather;
TV keens at audience; blank, cold room
nurses a dead pot of tea. The air stirs
with silence my mother will not break.
Nor I, who walk past her and out ...
into the lonely world. Without affection,
I know I must never look back
into this memory: mirror; dark place.
To birth something as precious
as a child, then bear them to give up
is no grief at all, no way to surrender

goodbye   *goodbye*

is no grief at all, no way to surrender
a child. Give them up, then bear
to birth something as precious,
as dark and mirrored as this memory.
I know you will never look back,
the world lonely without affection
as you walk past me and out ...
of a silence you will not break. Daughter
of dead air, stir empty tea-pot, nurse
cold room, keen audience of blank TV.
White sheet out in bad weather,
you are built of things already lost.
The revenant-like remains
of home and memory last
forever as you leave me.

My Mother is a Ghost Living in My Mind

The dead aren't always buried.
Some live on in silence   separated
by their need to
                                 slip
                                          away. To me,
she is forever cold, as if lost
at sea or in undying snowstorm, body
seized by fog or mind disturbed
from collective memory. 'Who are you?'
I ask, 'Where did you go?'

One moment, a farewell;
the next, a refusal to speak: she
comes to me in crises, plagues
the absent days and nights of
Lockdown until, darkness upon me,
I call down the heavens to end it all.

The other life I might have known
with her is filament burned
into my mind. A movie
never released; a book
unpublished: these I inherit
as she ghosts me. The forgeries
and false antiques of reconciliation,
long-lost phone calls stirring
in the still of night, I learn
to surrender everything in time.

When finally free, hope is broken-
winged and blunt-billed. Downed
by careful navigation and deceit,
I'm left to the emptiness
of another, to embalm and burden
myself, her silence and haunting
judgement born by me as eternal cut.

The Ghostwriter's Life is a Translated Poem

Transposed, word
for word, bone
to bone, something's
lost. As if a body –
daughter, friend or lover –
disappears into the night,
wakes elsewhere, stranger,
enemy or intruder,
speaks of its origin, not
its new beginning.

The freedom to move
from one state to
another isn't found

in the hard or torn
heart, the tongue
made indecipherable
or the editing out of self.

No, it's in the translation,
how it holds meaning,
how tears still spill
off the page, pooling
as blood. No crime, this
migration, this movement of
blood and being across space.

I'm relocated into the world
of my other half, our offspring,
our reproductions, a building
they call home. The clock ticks,
seconds shucked; the skin of
feet and metre peeled back
and stitched into another.

In this way, time passes;
I retrace the same story
in form and reflection
as its spectral remains.

Ghost Poem

*After Reading Harvey Bashion's 'The Migrant Lives in the
Haunted House of the Past'**

The window is an unforgiving friend.
It holds me in. It swallows my sky,

banishes strangers, neighbours
and those who get too close. Gone

elsewhere like migratory birds. Gone
to fearful spaces beyond, like the dead.

Now my days are full with such distraction
as settles me. Unquestioning as faith,

I observe the sanctity of ceiling
and wall, the furniture of my life.

When night creeps in to wipe me away
with its insomnia, I become small

screams in a house. In the morning,
I return to the window of my world

as if to a poem I refuse
to complete. Here, think

of newspaper reports about civil war
in Syria and Yemen, migrants displaced

to oceans dark as granite and drugs
which enshrine dependency. A ghost

of someone I used to know disturbs
the window with their knocking, and I

am frozen to think this stranger
has come to commune with the glazed-

like thing I've become, the swallowed
sky reflecting my lack of light.

* A ghost poem is an invented form, a verse inspired by a poem and/
or poet who might – but doesn't – exist.

Ulysses Syndrome

*Immigrant Syndrome of Chronic and Multiple Stress is
experienced by those exposed to extreme levels of anxiety unique
to the process of modern migration*

I wake to darkness,
as if to a nightmare;
as if this is real:
the uncertainty of
surroundings, the need
to ask, am I home?

I turn to a clock,
tired digits disturbed
by movement,
the bed I lie in,
an unfamiliar room,
and feel my bones ache
to rise, like sails, and glide
through hours lost elsewhere,
another homeland, another time.

When I'm taken back
by sleep, it is to relive
my past as if it's my future,
my future as if it's my past.

Beyond the walls
of the life, the home
I've rebuilt, some animal
stalks the wilderness, and I
follow it, in search of being
nowhere and nobody,
number, not name,
imposter, not impressive,
pariah, not person.

A fragment of
another dream, I wake
to belonging as a ghost
ship adrift in bad weather;
and I'm also the storm,
and I'm also the deep.

All that survives
is my memory, flowering
open and golden in its skin,
yesterday as the fruit of
many bruises and scarring
words. Until it's dead,
almost, a parent
who disowns me,
old friend and new lover
broken by the oxygen
of my phantom-like air.

So breathe in, breathe out,
as if an iron lung. I become,
in this way, able to survive
the trick of waking to darkness,
uncertain in its surroundings;
as if to a nightmare,
as if to myself.

Someone Other than Myself

They are but dressings of a former sight – SHAKESPEARE, SONNET CXXIII

And now autumn draws close, the ghost of
the woman and country I was resurfaces
like the seasons, to haunt lives and landscapes
I've left behind; such memories, such grief.

This is what happens to those who migrate. Time
continues unchanged as someone other than myself
takes their first breath, watches my plane inhale
the sky, returns to my apartment, their footsteps
upon its wooden floor echoing in my heart. Mirror;

writing desk; writing paper; the bed I slept late in:
these furnish their soul as well as my own. As I
arrive on foreign soil, they write an elegy. As I
wed, they compose a sonnet. As my son is born,
their collection delivers them the Forward Prize.

Yet this is what I miss most: my anorexia and abuse revived
by someone other than myself; the parents who rejected
me reconciled to someone other than myself. Nothing
novel; nothing strange. Tomorrow I'll return to the place
– an old street, an old house – I left. Ajar, an old door

will disclose an old mirror holding a reflection of someone
other than myself as footsteps, echoes in the heart, draw close.

My First Boyfriend is an Apparition of the Heart

Sometimes the sun doesn't set
upon a shadow. A tendril of something
survives, stretching across time. Like
how he didn't look like a lover
of poetry; like, *In you the rivers sing
and my soul flees in them,** never
slipped from his lips. He tasted not
of oysters or figs, cared little for
champagne. Eau Savage was not
his fragrance. His was not a jawline raw
as razor cut, and he didn't wear to-die-for
leather jacket, drainpipes or sleek Calvin Kleins.

No, in those days when girls were persuaded
to true love found in *Some Kind of Wonderful*,
Move Closer and *The House of the Spirits*, he

cut heroin, and surfed,
smelt of Old Spice and smoked,
tasted of salt, and his body was
a loose set of knives. He came
with no warning, no protection.

And so we kissed and the rest …
And this is why he'll always be the first
to *tastesmelltouchappearandsound* of loss
that night, fine as thread, as a yarn
about the-one-and-only, something
inside me   inside him   broke
like a mirror, like the heart
snatched back.

* 'Ah Vastness of Pines' by Pablo Neruda (*Twenty Love Poems and a Song of Despair*, London: Jonathan Cape, 1969, p. 13)

Listening to David Sylvian, the Ghostwriter Considers the Past

I belong to the past. Like the spirit
belongs to the scream, like music

to the instrument and air. *The room*
is quiet, the daylight almost gone ... *

The past lives remotely, nomad
whose return flight I must pay for.

It is unpredictable as turbulence
when close and cruel again, a childhood relived,

not in the moment but its recurrent scars:
the sallow and stomach-pumped casualty

of a mother's medication, the lost complaint;
blackouts and reprimands revisiting each abuse,

the hushed whispers on how to leave no damage;
the dark case hauled into the light, the last train

stealing me away, no tearful farewell, no
phone rung until dead, just 'Good riddance

to bad rubbish!' thundering down the years. Almost
palpable, this past I ache to ghost. Not alone;

we all possess remnants we want erased. Life,
reduced to the present, seems simpler; so

where's the harm? ... *the doubt inside my mind comes*
and goes but leads nowhere ... Sometimes we disappear

'Search' histories or 'Facebook' friends.
Sometimes we are the disappeared. In fault-

system and erosion, the land sets free its past.
Earthquake, hurricane and eruption: delete.

Cardiac arrest, disappearance and suicide: delete.
Yet in open vein, absence and arrhythmia, memory

survives. In magma, storm and rupture, memory
survives. Even the infirm body, weak of heart,

buried and decomposed, endures. Silent,
yet perpetual as a god, the past –

my troubled companion – never abandons me.
The ghosts of my life blew wilder than the wind …

The storm ravages its landscape. The rogue
wave upends its craft. But there is renewal.

So I call upon the past to return, again
and again to do its worst, and resurrect me.

* all italicised words are lyrics from 'Ghosts' by Japan, 1981

The Parents Considered as Invisible Remains

I'm a body in need of new heart.
They're phantom limbs still feeling pain.

I'm an accident and the only one to blame.
They're torture and the bodies I must bury.

I'm the flight that keeps them grounded.
They're the memory that keeps me misplaced.

I'm an empty space in their home.
They're a lost cause in my opinion.

I'm the curse in their spells of outrage.
They're the spite in my spells of self-harm.

I'm their language of silence, bruises and scars.
They're my reason for poetry, beats and breaks.

We're cross-leases, neighbours at war.
We're bad debts, bailiffs at the door.

We're a shelter, braced against each other.
We're a building, four walls and a roof of pain.

Ghost Words

for Cameron

Ghost word: a meaningless word mistakenly published and republished in a dictionary

Dord – I want it to define 'Dad', not
as ghost word, density. The magnitude of
you, Dord, in my life, I want anchored
not in your absence but in your closeness,
not in your hardness but in your gentleness.
In volume as exact as it is imprecise,
I want you, Dord, to love me as I am,
not as you need me to be. Atomic number;
negative valence; burden of your disdain: no,
I want to say, Dord, you matter to me.

Feamyng – I want it to define 'Mum', not
as ghost word, busyness or mistake.
I want the brisk shifts in its evolution to be,
like a family, something which belongs to me.
Busyness, besyness, fesynes: the heart opens out
like mother, grandma, great-grandma, a ripening
rediscovery of the self. Out of our silence,
I want to say, Feamyng, I'm not your mistake,
for what we are isn't what we might have been:
sisters, nurturers and mothers, close as words.

Peckage – I want it to define, my son,
the language of your childhood, not
the meaningless babble of a babe. Not
in density or busyness or mistake; but
a treasured memory of motherhood,
as a word which means I love you. Gift:
when you are grown, my son,
I will hand it down

to you
and your children
and their children
our ancestry yours
to edit, rephrase
as the ghost words of me
are
slowly
erased

Dord, ghost word, def: density (*Webster's New International Dictionary*, II edn);
Feamyng, ghost word, def: busyness of ferrets (*Oxford English Dictionary*);
Peckage, ghost word, def: chicken (Harvey-Doherty crib talk)

If Befriending Ghosts

If they are the legacy left in lost code
If they are the beginning of broken soul

If they are the bitter end of love
If they are the sour taste of rejection

If they are the other side of the story
If they are the curses cast into oblivion

If they are the chemical rendering of light
If they are the sky at the point of breaking

If they are a house troubled by occupants
If they are a dwelling upon difficult territory

If they are my crying out of pain
If they are my tearing open old wounds

If they are my looking deep inside
If they are my viscera, blood and bile

I will give them oxygen and time
I will give them fuel and flame

I will raise them to ruin, to wreck
I will raise them as lovers, as pets

I will wear them up like a leash
I will wear them down to a dust

I will be their armour, their second skin
I will be their padded cell, their asylum

Safe Places for Ghosts

*The ache for home lives in all of us, the safe place where we can
go as we are and not be questioned.*

MAYA ANGELOU

Other Bodies

Ghost of air, migrant of water, exile of earth land
here: in the bodies of others. As if a dwelling,

each is skin to own. As if alien,
each is carved in bone. All memories

made here bleed into you. All the forgotten
await at the tip of your new tongue.

With renewed voice, whisper new secrets.
With restored health, cauterize old wounds;

heal. This is the miracle of being
given a second chance. This is a dream

detached from its nightmare. Stay safe
in the knowledge, you're no longer

painted as something you are not.
When ghost, migrant and exile of

other bodies seek shelter here, move on.
For now, this is life; make the most of it.

Shelter

A
kindred
spirit of air
water earth ghost
shelter here in space
tight as reflection swallowing
door room floor window & roof
enough to build a back-up life all light
& dark all decoration disposable & damage
fusing into you as if transplant or iron lung
collapsing   like death   collapsing
into ether   **like door**   into cloud
like invisible **open**   **close** as suburbia
the highway **open**   **close** the inroads
deep current **open**   **close** narrow tide
this buoyant **open**   **close** this settled

The Future is a Place of Rest

And in the future no more unpredictable human hazards
– BBC CLICK, 'Rise of the Machines'

God, never let this pen write about the steady fall of rain. Never
let it mark autumn's arrival with the cold tick of a clock. Always

allow it to avoid mention of autonomous mechanisms, artificial
intelligence, programmable matter, utility fog … The clouding of

such certainties as will soon swamp us, mirror and make us
redundant isn't what poetry is for. A poem is not an algorithm.

It does not possess 'goal function', or specification – unreasoning
and obvious as light – on how a problem must be solved. No,

a poem is reasoned by the teardrop, the quivering lip and the heart
astonished by its own arrhythmia or unexpected attack. All that

circuitry of story. Simple impulse. Simple wireless communication.
This is why those superfluous to the future find refuge here.

Spectres of the past: they will reappear to our descendants –
designed out of evolution – whenever the poem is read.

Resilience in its most erratic form. Already the future composes
metrical schemes of industry cleansed of capricious human creativity.

God, what a fix! Let it be disturbed by the poems yet to awaken
empty pages. Let it be erased by the poems keeping the lost alive.

They are dormant protests. They are questions waiting to be asked.
And like resistance and doubt, just words. Again and again,

let this pen return with irregularity to its craft. God, build this poem
into others as a legacy which will work differently from the rest.

The Architecture of the Poem

Remember everything is made of air.
Architecture is the impossible science
of flight, sets human and ghost loose
to dance in deep space, the exiled
free to sail the heavens like cloud.

A poem too relies upon navigation
with an absence made concrete.
The foundations are elsewhere, invisible.
Like Bauhaus and Corbusier, the form is
aesthetic composition, music to behold.

Think of the bearing, of the weight
measured in meaning and pitch. Think
words create lines solid as weatherboard,
create stanzas which breathe as bodies,
as shells. Hear the sound, structurally safe.

So move in; furnish it with the familiar
and strange, the solid and fragile. Here light
illusions are windows with new perspectives;
the reflections beyond. Here, like a rainbow,
live open to the elements, live almost in the sky.

The Ghost in the Library

It's built from embers of inspiration. The ghost,
among them, discovers the afterworld of books.
Finds Eliot in *The Waste Land*, Milton in *Paradise
Lost*; Asimov in *The Stars, Like Dust. The Sleeper
Awakes* in Wells. Heaney opens *Door into the Dark* …

The ghost walks through these eternities,
as if their walls are smoke or filament almost
burnt out. Distant comets pass through ether
here. Pinpricks of light are impossible reminders
of the last breath outlived; the luminous survive …

Such invisible artistry, the ghost is compelled
to complete other poems, novels and memoirs,
each fierce as a fire. A place to live, to hide;
the soul immersed in the story, something
enigmatic – a vestige – remaining after the end.

Among the Stars

a sequence

i: Here Among the Stars

At dusk, the nightclub pulses. Eyes alight
like sparks, like spirits. The heat as other bodies

dance close. Here find one another. Until *Bitter
Sweet Symphony* steals you outside. The sky is set

against first kiss. This is what it's like to discover
the coordinates of a constellation. The dark pelt

of a river carries you home. Snow drifts
in light bulb shards. Fireworks; lantern

festivals; midnight feasts: all you have is
the night, and how it turns you

to telescopes, needle-sharp compasses
and cool, tarmac hearts. Here is Crux,

your engagement; Gemini, your marriage.
Here also, in deep space, a collapse,

like the breaking of an egg.
The full rotation of a comet.

A star is newborn. As if by Pisces, a child
hauls you in. Now he's your brightest thing.

You watch over him while he sleeps.
When he wakes, he reflects your happiness.

When he moves
                   it's as if
                              he walks on
                                          cloud.

ii: Home Powered by Starlight

I always wanted you to go into space, man – Babylon Zoo

The walls respire like the skin of a balloon

The hallway is a row of ice-blue bodies

The kitchen is a heart beating with its occupants' storms

The staircase is a magic carpet made of minor planets

The bedroom is a breathing space for the imagination

The desk is full of cavities into which codes and star catalogues spill

The bookshelf is a supernova, brilliant in its explosions of light

The bed is a cloud of dust and dormant gas suspended in a violent dream

Here is a nightmare: being spun out to red-black shards

Here is a daydream: being lit like a ring of frost

Here is the staircase again, let it swallow you elsewhere

And the door? Open to dark matter; close to collapse

iii: Home Powered by Black Hole

A house is a physical thing, like the Sea
of Serenity and the Oceans of Storm.

It possesses the momentum of the tide
in the estuary, the dark undertow wrenching

matter in, cloud float, the passing song
of birds no longer able to nest, the fruit

on the branch rotting and summer's dying
heat, patient to the end. Ongoing story,

the old house occupies a moving place
in its surroundings, emptying all light

so that always its inhabitants might live
in darkness, eyes closed to the miracle

they inhabit. While the house continues
to chart coordinates of its own abyss.

iv: Dead Constellations

In stargazing, the sky is a place to dwell
in contemplation of how you might live
again in two dimensions, the electricity of
the present fused to the inertia of the past.

Apis, Cerberus, Noctua ... ancients emerge.
Hollow, their eyes search for family far away
settled warmly into new hearts, new names.

They know their faces are faint reflections
of how life came to be. In disappearing,
they imagine the dense body of home
vanishes for good, like messages
of hope written in invisible ink
erase the burden of an empty page.

Let Us Live Reborn

The Roman Bot – Outliers, BBC, 2/7/19 *

Not a traditional way to go.
A dead man delivered up
to the mobile phones of others –
troubled texts; memorable advice –
and downloaded, as if casket slipping
from the solid to the spectral.

Then brought back to life. You
predicted this, just as your words
are conjured into a clairvoyant
of sorts. For all algorithms and AI,
you process the grief friends feel
at your loss, their unrecoverable despair.

Then with care of counsellor or priest,
you offer ether-healing and absolution.
Raise profound questions too. Like:
can existence be reduced to a formula?
Can the living replicate the lost?
Can the dead speak? Are they real,
these conversations across silent space?

While we work out the answers, you
continue to have your say, leaving us
to our memories. Poetry-sharp soundbites
screening in the mind, they reconnect us
to the cellular existence of you.

* When Moscow cultural event organiser and influencer Roman
Mazurenko died, his friends decided to keep his memory alive by
creating a digital monument, a bot of him which allowed those who
knew him to text and converse with him.

The Ghost Resurrects the Family

Haunting it from within, all ghosts –
disappeared, departed and displaced –
find solace in the family they create;
as in a new home. For them, to parent
is to raise the dead and breathe fresh air
into ancient rites of passage. All
for their children, their future.
So that they will never know
how to grow invisible. Never see
the hardships of the hand-me-downs:
worn shoes; torn clothes; broken toys;
taunts; cold baths; half-finished meals.

The bodies never embraced; the words
never spoken: these too the ghost fades
from its offsprings' lives. Of course,
the damaged always loiter somewhere
out of reach. Like knives; clear cut
crystal; diamond ring: all pledged
as inheritance, to be passed down
as silently as curly hair and anaemia.
But the ghost doesn't bleed out all
its harm; who does? The kids are safe
to make their own mistakes:
the ghost is at peace with that.

To Live in a Telephone Box

Kaze no denwa: the wind phone installed in Otsuchi, northern Japan, after the 2011 tsunami, for the grieving to communicate with the dead

Here is the unspoken spirit of you,
a connection which grief manifests
as a white, glass-panelled box.

Vault open to the receiver;
raise to invoke the spectre of
what was and will never be said.

And if it voices anything, it is loss,
our communion with a severed line.

As if the dead
stand in another place, always
on hold, awaiting our call.
And when we're put through
to all the things we've held onto
because we can't hold onto you,
there's such release, like rain,
like the sky cleansed of storm.

Still we imagine the whether,
why, what, where and if.

Still we imagine all uncertainties:
ancestors unknown; disembodied
names written in letters from the past.

Soon the earth will call back,
the voices of the buried
will rise up, songs of refrain.

Until then, all this revealed here
strengthens the weight of silence,
the ghosts of conversations
lost, the secrets long kept.

So lips pursed, deadened, we
steal to listen, as if tuning into
a misplaced frequency, eternal
in our waiting for this, for you
to say hello, to say our names.

The Wide, Open Spaces

Let us shelter in their beginnings:
the silence before first scream;
the darkness before eyes open;
the absence before bowels excrete.

Let us shelter in their characterisation:
the body about to discover movement;
the blank textbook awaiting the lesson;
the teenage rebel cut from the crowd.

Let us shelter in their narrative arc:
the room where the writer sits alone;
the second before inspiration strikes;
the rough draft of the finished work.

Let us shelter in their subtext:
the meaning below the surface, shadow
prowling deep water; the shallow pulse
of a heart broken – caesura – by its beat.

Let us shelter in their endings:
the lungs releasing last breath;
the sun setting at shut-eye;
the final page torn from a book.

Epilogue

Poem, a Place Where Regeneration is Complete

Soul haunting its space, the writer returns
to the final poem. As if a sleight of hand,
a draft teases open a door, a clock turns
to witching-hour. Shadow at the back: this
the writer senses as they divine a double-
meaning, add alliteration, revise a line
break, then realise an end-

                            stop.
Here are ways to close out the poem:
tide high in the estuary, a boat rocks
a luckless fisherman, finally a catch; hauling
belongings, the displaced reappear, spirit
activists standing their ground; a refrain of
owl, bittern and black cormorant; a shiver of
sharks making for the deep. The sanctuary of
the writer's imagination hosts all conclusions,
then abandons them. Outside something is off-
leash and prowling streets lit by a waxing moon.
Night moves towards

                         its finale. The writer relives
upset: *Community not opportunity!*, *Give us back
our homes!* ... sirens and teargas, the ghosts of
empty houses, raised skywards and floating
elsewhere ... such things as seem no more
than footnotes or epilogues to those living
in a place where regeneration is complete.
At the edge of

                     awakening, they stir with
thoughts of curtains about to open, life-
stories about to unfold. In fits 'n' starts,
the writer sits with the incomplete
poem as with a clairvoyant, channelling
matter they thought misplaced ... until
fresh ideas emerge. Like sudden rain,
they feed arid terrain. Clouds tremble.

Rooftops sing. Soul haunting its space,
the writer settles to resolve their work.
A few droplets
                fall as words
breathe life into
                the poem's last line.

Afterword

Living in the Haunted House of the Past: or Renovation, Writing and How to Construct a Living Room While Searching for a Home

One need not be a chamber to be haunted – EMILY DICKINSON

This is a house, my first since settling in the city, an escape from my parents, my past: a narrow single-storey frame, a shell composed into existence in the 1930s by a man called Savage who saw in it, and its replication countrywide, space for the overlooked and struggling to enjoy a better life; its placement in the crook of a bay, which affords a panorama over fluctuating estuary and wide sky, dramatic in their transient performances, is a location many of my neighbours have paid millions of dollars for, even though the outlook doesn't belong to anyone; four tight rooms, all without doors, which I pass through as if a ghost; a floor that raises me above the solidity of the earth, floating me in space; a roof that masquerades as a tattered crown a functionary might wear to make themselves seem significant while they administer their temporary role; the whole thing held together, like my body, by heart and mind, those pieces of personal architecture I know have function and meaning but ultimately are fleeting tricksters, a moment from collapse.

*

This is also a house. Like smoke, memories of childhood drift through my mind. They seem as chimerical, as unanchored as the place where I now reside. From this distance, measured in decades as much as in kilometres, what endures most in my memory of the house I lived in until I was seventeen, is its skin.

The houses in the long, twisted street where I grew up were replicas of each other. Semi-detached boxes, four rooms upstairs, four rooms downstairs, dropped onto small squares of land. Colloquially, they were named after their builder, George Wimpey, who mass-produced them to house lower-working-class families across the industrial heart of England.

The peculiarity of the house where I lived lay in its placement. There was a dogleg in the street, and the dwelling that was built on the inside of the curve – ours – was different from the rest. The other houses, constructed to front the road, presented one face to the world, whereas our section bordered the curvature of the street and our house presented both front and side. It was, in a term that now seems apt, two-faced.

*

He appears, like recollections of my childhood house, at a time of inactivity.

The trouble is I'm not writing. An author is a tenant always at the mercy of a harsh landlord, their muse. It's a year since my last book was published. The days since have seen me try, but fail, to inhabit other projects, other ideas.

Into this fallow expanse my builder, Scott, fan of Coelho's *The Alchemist* after which he has named his business, arrives.

I need a new living room. I need a place that might possess the sea, mountain and air, that expensive panorama beholden to no one. So Scott starts to eviscerate my house.

*

Did I see, in the irregular position of that dwelling of my childhood, a mirror of my own difference? Before I could create a language – a poetry – to articulate my feelings of disconnection from home and family, did this house, frail in its uniform casing, slight as its glassy windows, replicate my unease?

Perhaps. Perhaps not.

The sanctuary a house can provide, whether it's formed in ill-symmetry or otherwise, is never composed exclusively of its shape or shell. That house, like every house, was substance physical and experiential. Within its higgledy-piggledy carapace it was – and lingers so in my recollection – the sum parts of so many things: everyday experiences and dysfunctions; relationships; emotions; memories. Interlaced, these meant that the house, through no fault of its own, could never provide safety enough to be called home.

*

A morning early in the construction: when alchemist Scott arrives with a worn-out copy of Pablo Neruda's *The Book of Questions* and his tools, I ask him, 'Where's home?'

Lyrically, he speaks of rural life in the Waikato, Elysium-like pastures and parents who love him.

Such a sheltered life, I think, dismissively; what does he know?

'But,' he adds, 'it's also elsewhere.' The Sun Gate at Machu Picchu; las casas in Cartagena where balconies flower with bougainvillea; Torres del Paine, Patagonia: he dwells on highlights of a South American OE. 'And, of course, Casa de Isla Negra, Valparaiso,' he exclaims, pointing to *The Book of Questions*, as if this says it all.

*

A memory of the residence of my youth displaces me: a time when summer's dry air and suffocating heat breach closed window, drawn drapes and locked door. It is 5pm, the room dazzling with light no nylon curtain can subdue. Sound spills in as children outside play chase and hopscotch; the screech, sweet as birdcall, of bike tires tearing along the asphalt; skipping games, girls singing, 'A sailor went to sea, sea, sea/ To see what he can see, see, see …'

They have knocked at our door, these children, to ask if I can play. But Mrs Y is having none of it. All morning and afternoon locked inside while a prolonged downpour refreshed thirsting grass, my endless noise and the sound of my toys clattering against floor and wall have roused Mrs Y into bitter admonishments and beatings.

Now the deluge has stopped and Mr Y has left for his nightshift, a tired Tupperware box hiding cheese sandwiches, a weary flask of tea under his arm, another nocturnal crafting of mechanical parts ahead of him. Mrs Y is left alone with me. Without dinner, I'm hustled into bed, told to go to sleep or else, the door closed, so she can sit in my silence with a Vesta 'Boil in the Bag' chow mein meal and restful thoughts.

My seven-year-old body, feverish in its energy, aches to open the window and fly outside …

I imagine the sky, warm and delicately crimson in late summer heat, backdrop to me, my friend Karen and our games of make-believe houses, an old sheet framing our domain, dolls and a chipped toy tea set indulging us in our play …

This longing slips me through closed doors, scurries me into Mr and Mrs Y's bedroom, where I settle before a window open to free the oppressive heat. From there I watch young bodies dance in and out of a skipping rope as it spins in ripe air. There also I hear laughter and ongoing song, 'But all that he could see, see, see/ Was the bottom of the deep blue sea, sea, sea …'

From below, Mrs Y's growl rises like fire. Footsteps scorch the stairs.

I race back to my room, close the door, lie in fake slumber beneath heavy blankets. I feel my eyelids tighten as Mrs Y crashes in. Then there's the barking, 'I SAID, GO TO SLEEP!' My breath quickens as she pulls back covers, presses her left hand into my back, flattens me against the inflexible mattress while her right hand readies the belt. The lashes that reign down empty me, tears and blood spilling in silence until I'm hollow.

*

It takes a week for Scott to turn my laundry and hallway into a husk. That part of the house – facing the deep, the jagged ranges and the wild sky – once a dim washroom and cramped corridor, vanishes, enduring only in the mind. Instead, shadows remain upon the floor, tracing memories of where walls once rested.

Seeing them, I retire to the rear of the house where, because of the renovation, my bedroom idles as a transitory space in which to sleep, eat, read and contemplate. Against the symphony of Scott's saw and hammer, I sit before a ream of blank paper as, ghost-like, a few lines of something materialise.

'Momentarily, I look upon these frail outlines as if upon a vision: not the bones of something about to be born, but a fallen body, a crime scene …'

*

'I SAID, GO TO SLEEP!'

When I wake an hour or so later, these haunting words befriend sharp pain. The light has lowered. The sound of children outside is a dying refrain.

I wince as I creep downstairs, the prickle of my welted skin as keen as the realisation that I'm alone in the house, the back door open. I sneak to the step, spy Mrs Y cutting the sated front lawn with a hand mower, her face impassive as she refuses the glare of neighbouring parents who sweep yards and wash cars.

Karen is one of the few kids still outside. She sees me, waves but doesn't smile. It's enough to meet her eye, to be seen by her and to feel her warmth before I sneak a cup of water, satisfy an unbelievable thirst then make the slow climb, each step accompanied by invisible barbs to my body, back to the room with its drawn curtains and blood-stained bed.

*

While Scott labours, I continue to write. An anechoic chamber in my head banishes the grating of the Mitre saw and punch of the hammer, as half-memory, half-imagination, more lines emerge.

'There's a mystery here, where I hadn't seen one before, an arcane power to deliver evidence from invention …'

*

With its violence, spite, bickering and conditional love, Mr and Mrs Y's dwelling was an imitation – a simulacra – of the abodes constructed for them to reside in when they were young.

The ghosts of those places, houses haunted by inherited abuse, linger in me. They congregate, second selves, in my mind.

I can almost inhabit my parents' memories of them.

Here's the edifice of the house Mrs Y was raised in. Its rooms – naked floors, grey walls, slight furniture – are decorated with a poverty that exceeds the one I knew as a girl. Two bedrooms: five boys in one, four girls in the other; the departed soul of baby Patricia, lost to pneumonia, cowers in the corner. A third room, cramped by a single bed, accommodates the parents. Thirteen-year-old Mrs Y inherits the task of housekeeping this residence the day after she receives a letter informing her parents that she's one of only two students in her year to be offered a place at grammar school. I can almost see the spectre of her father, a callous grin to his maw as he shreds that invitation to academia, that escape from the destitution and constraint of this dwelling. He faces her down as he informs her that she won't be going back to school. Instead he constructs an alternative future in which her remaining youth is demolished by scrubbing floors, polishing cheap furniture, making tired beds, preparing all meals and cleaning all clothes, while her mother, thinned out by working four jobs, slowly succumbs to cancer, and he – that tiny, violent, chain-smoking, yellowed man – whiles away his mornings gardening before squandering his wife's wages in the betting shop on long shots and nags.

And here, separate yet somehow conjoined like a shadow to Mrs Y's childhood residence, is my mind's spectral delineation of the house Mr Y grew up in. A puzzling form. It seems almost normal, this place he shares with his mother, grandmother and grandfather, all of whom idolise him. Not this: the unspoken-of boarding home in Blitz-besieged Britain, circa 1941, to which my unwed grandmother might have been confined during her third trimester. No, not this: the foster home Mr Y might have been sequestered to, and there abandoned. Instead, Mr Y's childhood residence was a welcoming place, built so by his deeply pious grandparents, who refused the mores of a time that determined that an infant born out of wedlock, with no acknowledged father, should be rejected.

The problem with this almost idyllic depiction of Mr Y's childhood house is its invisibility. The address, the site of unconditional love and nurturing grandparents, was never spoken of, so stymied was Mr Y by his illegitimacy. It was my uncle, fathered by another man, who a few years ago let slip the existence of the property. In doing so he unwittingly and belatedly dismantled the last attachments I held to the house Mr Y colluded to compose for me, the one where walls were lined with conditional love, brutality and mutilations; where, even at the end, my suitcase at the door, the final words Mr Y delivered were callous and unimaginative: 'Good riddance to bad rubbish!'

*

Scott measures out the dimensions of my new living room and marks them in chalk upon dusty floorboards. Momentarily, I look upon these frail outlines as if upon a vision: not the bones of something about to be born, but a fallen body, a crime scene. There's a mystery here, where I hadn't seen one before, an arcane power to deliver evidence from invention, to make inspiration concrete through the slogged-out realisation of something aesthetic, transformative and unique.

My eye returns to the lifeless chalk outline. Such erasure; such power to resurrect.

I slip back to my improvised workspace, where more words appear.

*

There's a point in the writing process that always feels most spectral to me: the mid-point, that liminal space between beginning and uncertain completion.

I'm writing an essay; as more sentences have emerged, I've come to realise this. Yet the cohesion of this extended work, all settled and fully mended, still eludes me, and this makes me feel exposed, unsettled.

I turn to the wise counsel of other writers, particularly poets who are also essayists, like Billy Collins and Mary Oliver.

I read a transcript of a discussion Collins gave about structure. It begins:

> *I am always aware that I'm writing something which is at least tidy, at least shaped in some way and that is both a box for the poem to live in and it's also the container that will embrace the reader when he or she is reading the poem ...*[1]

I find room in my thinking for his advice on how to attain shape in the form of a finished piece. He calls on authors to use their eyes as much as their ears when writing. Here, he says, is a means for the work to attain an aesthetic symmetry on the page. In his opinion, lines of verse should provide horizontal support, their consistent lengths composing shape and solidity; stanzas

---

1 *Billy Collins: On the road with the Poet Laureate*, Richard B. Woodward (director), 2003, (DVD).

should be arranged in patterns, their lines numerically similar.

I see an architecture in Collins' approach, a way to incorporate his advice into my essay and so give it a presence on the page. Thereafter, as I construct paragraphs into sections, I consider their careful placement in white space and, through adaptation, how their intersections with each other might complete a durable whole.

*

Once more my childhood house emerges like a reclamation, an act of recycling memory and self. Winter, the sky darkening as the evening news, in amplification, awakens me to factory closures and monstrous unemployment rates. Then the prime minister appears offering the phantom of hope: a Right to Buy scheme which, it's determined, will create a nation of homeowners.

It sounds like a disaster to me, millions of people burdened with debt – financial, experiential, memorial, ancestral – that will never be discharged.

But what do I know?

At that moment, burning like a fuse, Mrs Y returns from her minimum-wage shift in a wallpaper shop. Once settled to her seat in front of the fire she launches into a tirade about my failures: dinner not prepared on time or to her liking; my disappointing school grades ...

I'm fourteen and, as captives often do, have normalised her abusive, depressive personality and Mr Y's reticent, largely absent disposition; their dysfunctions and the squalid site of their control. My coping strategies include pretending, along with the neighbours, that everything is a commonplace façade; not answering back; passing out when punched, and hiding bruises and scars.

But tonight, whether through the attrition of living with all this, the decade-long suppression of something I can't name, or simply being a powerless teenager hungry for the possibility of adulthood elsewhere, I charge towards my bedroom at the top of the house where, in utter darkness, I scream. The sound and habitation of my voice surprises me. That such power and pain live inside me, have done so for so long, building, building … this is an occupancy, an agency I didn't know I owned.

Then the door breaks open like a wave. With nothing more than a fist and an energy born of a need to erase anything that might incite the neighbours to break rank and phone the police, Mrs Y knocks me to the floor, falls to her knees and continues the beating. Only when I'm reduced to a whimper no one but Mrs Y can hear does she stop.

The door closes.

Darkness complete.

*

At night when Scott lays down tools and vacates the reconstruction, I scour and cleanse. Always there's a film of grime like old skin (mine or another's?), which must be removed. At sink, floor and window, the growing darkness draws me to remove the stains I see, the stains I don't.

Later, as I lie in bed listening to the patient breathing of the house, I consider what ownership – of this place where I write, this place I'm rebuilding – confers upon me. Does it give me protection from the troubles of my upbringing? Does it sever my link to Mr and Mrs Y? Or – an act of ultimate irony– does it make me a mirror of my parents? Having escaped their tortuous abode, determined never to be like them, have I taken possession of something that to all intents and purposes is a replica of them?

*

The aftermath of any cruelty involving Mrs Y is usually the same: I steal downstairs, bruised and injured, to find her reclining on a rug before a brutal blaze. She seems lost to some kitchen-sink drama flickering on the television. I approach, kneel, kiss her on the cheek and whisper, just loud enough for her to hear, 'sorry'. Mrs Y says nothing, her gaze fixed elsewhere as if I don't exist.

But this time it's as if stains emerge, like contusions, upon the wallpaper of the house. After indulging Mrs Y in her ceremony I retreat to my room where, for the remaining two years of my existence in this dwelling, I eat my meals, complete my homework and spend my sleeping hours imprisoned in a nightmare about an isolated manor, derelict and possessed.

*

Weeks pass as I draft my essay. While Scott measures Gib, cuts holes for new power points, dry-fits sheeting then glues and nails it in place, I turn to Mary Oliver's 'Building the House': 'Whatever a house is to the heart and body of man – refuge, comfort, luxury – surely it is as much and more to the spirit …'[2]

Her prose poetic, Oliver carries me through the journey of building a writing cabin. Along the way she meditates upon the art of constructing edifice and creative work. In her measured, lyrical writing style the two become fused, mirrors of a desire, a need to craft.

'Building the House' is an extended poem as much as an essay, the author's supple language teasing out double meanings and evoking parallels.

Finishing it, I perceive a way to complete my own essay, to strengthen meaning by furnishing the work with poetry's limberness and lilt.

*

Another disturbance, a sleep-shard of a lost life, plagues me. In this haunting, the walls of an unfamiliar hideaway are lined with glass yet offer me no reflection, so that I'm unable to locate myself or determine where I belong.

This and other traumas become so frequent and fantastical while Scott renovates and I revise multifarious drafts of my essay, that I begin to believe there's purpose here: memory, dream, reconstruction and writing as remnants of some threadbare myth, oddities locked into make-believe space where something insignificant must be spun into something precious.

*

---

2 'Building the House', in *Upstream: Selected essays* by Mary Oliver (New York: Penguin, 2016), p. 160.

Piqued by remembrance of Mrs Y's father, I spend a morning on ancestry.com.

As Scott stops joints, applies compound and tape to near-finished walls and rough-sands them, I seek to locate the nature of my grandfather's birth. He who thwarted Mrs Y's dreams of learning. He of the ashen, tobacco-addicted form.

Scott is in the midst of his smoko, a cup of strong coffee close by, *The Book of Questions* replaced by Neruda's earlier *Extravagaria*, when my grandfather's birth certificate appears: 'Father – Unknown'.

*

Unknown, but not alone. Those great-grandparents I never met, who doted on their grandson, my father, and bravely rejected their era's abandonment of the illegitimate, preferring to hold their heads high in public even when hearing whispers in the pews and on neighbours' doorsteps. That devout, tender couple. What did they look like? More eludes me: the sounds of their voices, the smell of his newly ironed shirts fresh for Sunday service, or the taste of the roasts she laboured over.

Does writing live somewhere, a sanctuary, in the bodies and minds of my unknowable relatives? Somewhere within this misplaced whakapapa, is there an ancestor who was an author? Was the haven I find in words also found in their erased selves?

*

Eyes sharpened by scanning lines of Neruda's verse (*y así te espero como casa sola/ I wait for you like a lonely house*),[3] Scott knows the pace of building isn't always even. The scope of the renovation, the tearing down of old walls and construction of a new area, requires new flooring. His work is nearing the end when he fetches me to inspect a flaw. It lies in a delivery of fifty bevel-backed radiata pine floorboards. The timber is threaded green with rot, the result of the wood not being covered adequately during a squall.

---

3 'LXV', *100 Love Sonnets* by Pablo Neruda (Austin: University of Texas Press, 1999), p. 138.

Justin, the timber supply representative, arrives to investigate the problem.

'I quite like the green, don't you?' he says, somewhat naively.

Scott and I do not. If left, the defect will spread, tainting all and compromising the integrity of the new space. The flawed timbers are replaced with fresh, faultless lengths of *Pinus radiata*, which Scott nails in place then varnishes golden.

*

I'm nearing the end of the essay when my builder knocks on the door to tell me the living room is complete.

There I take in the glistening floor, the walls a warm yellow called 'Bright Spark',[4] the varnished skirting boards, the spectacular outlook – the one that stretches elsewhere. As I walk around the room, inhabit it, its emptiness reverberates with a longing for books, furniture, photographs and life.

There's something about the echo of my footsteps, though, that causes me to feel momentary doubt. I wonder if any building can ever be a shelter to me. If not, then what else is there? Is my body, that site built of blood, bone and brain, that site I liberated from Mr and Mrs Y's house, the only dwelling I possess?

Perhaps. Perhaps not.

As I survey my living room anew, I marvel at the undeniable artistry of Scott's work. The window frames, walls and floor: all hold a symmetry crisp as any song sheet. Like an image-cluster, they magnify the priceless view: settled water, expansive sky and nest of imposing cloud. I see now that this is more than a place to exist. This living room is a refuge where I can commune with word, form, metre, music and story, those elements of my being that – as unattainable as the origins of my need to write – predate the haunted house of my childhood. Yes, this living room is a window to sit at as I gaze into the changeable nature of my surroundings and discover inspiration for new work.

---

4 Resene Bright Spark, Colour Code: 2BY45.

Acknowledgements

I acknowledge being awarded the 2020 New Zealand Society of Authors Peter and Dianne Beatson Fellowship. I'm grateful for the support it offered in helping me complete this book.

I'm also grateful to the editors of the following magazines and anthologies in which some of these poems or versions of them first appeared: *Arc* (Ca); *Bonsai: Best small stories from Aotearoa New Zealand* (Canterbury University Press, 2018); *broadsheet 23 & 26*; *Cordite 80* (Aus); *Eucalisia* (It); *Flash Frontier*; *Fresh Ink: A collection of voices from Aotearoa New Zealand* (Cloud Ink, 2017); *Griffith Review* (Aus); *JAAM 33: Small departures*; *154 Poems by 154 Contemporary Poets in Response to Shakespeare's 154 Sonnets* (Live Canon, 2016); *Manifesto: 101 political poems* (Otago University Press, 2017); *Landfall*; *Not Very Quiet* (Aus); *Otago Daily Times*; *Poetry New Zealand 50*; *Poet's Republic* (Sco); *Scattered Feathers* (New Zealand Poetry Society, 2015); *Sobotka* (US); *Structo 15* (UK); *takahē*; *Take Back Our Sky* (New Zealand Poetry Society, 2014); *Tarot 1*; *Turbine\Kapohau*; *The Friday Poem*; *The Unnecessary Invention of Punctuation* (New Zealand Poetry Society, 2018).

A selection of these poems won the 2019 Kathleen Grattan Prize for a Sequence of Poems.

'Ghost Poem' and 'My Last Memory of Home' won the 2019 Dunedin UNESCO City of Literature Robert Burns Poetry Competition.

'The Evicted' and 'The State House Considered as a Ghost' were runners-up in the 2014 and 2015 New Zealand Poetry Society International Poetry Competitions.

'Living in the Haunted House of the Past' was placed third in the 2020 Landfall Essay Competition.

'The Future is an Unpredictable Place' was highly commended in the 2018 New Zealand Poetry Society International Poetry Competition.

'Building Memories' was long-listed for the 2019 *Australian Book Review* Peter Porter Prize.

'The Home Speaks' appeared publically on posters in New Zealand and the US as part of the Phantom Billstickers Poetry Project.

Deep gratitude is given to Rachel Scott for championing this book, to Paul and Briar for wise counsel while it was being drafted, and to Mr D and our amazing son, Cameron, for unwavering support. I also want to thank the rest of the team at Otago University Press: Laura Hewson, Imogen Coxhead and Fiona Moffat; and Emma Neale for her editing.